MARCY SCHAAF
AF421840
AGENT AVA
TOP SECRET MISSION

INTRODUCTION:
AGENT AVA, TOP SECRET MISSION

IN A BUSTLING CITY, WHERE SECRETS HIDE IN EVERY CORNER AND MYSTERIES ARE JUST WAITING TO BE UNCOVERED, LIVES AGENT AVA. BY DAY, SHE IS AN ORDINARY MOM, BUT BY NIGHT, SHE BECOMES A TOP-SECRET AGENT, TACKLING THRILLING MISSIONS AND SOLVING PERPLEXING PUZZLES. WITH HER TRUSTY WHITE SUV, HIGH-TECH GADGETS, AND HER QUICK THINKING, AVA IS ALWAYS READY FOR ACTION.

BUT TODAY IS DIFFERENT. TODAY, HER MISSION IS PERSONAL. IT'S HER DAUGHTER LILY'S BIRTHDAY, AND THE SPECIAL CUPCAKE AVA ORDERED HAS MYSTERIOUSLY DISAPPEARED. WITH THE CLOCK TICKING AND THE PARTY GUESTS ARRIVING, AGENT AVA MUST USE ALL HER SKILLS TO FIND THE MISSING CUPCAKE AND SAVE THE CELEBRATION.

JOIN AGENT AVA ON A HIGH-FLYING, FAST-DRIVING, AND LASER-CUTTING ADVENTURE IN **AGENT AVA, TOP SECRET MISSION**. IT'S A STORY OF BRAVERY, CLEVERNESS, AND THE LOVE BETWEEN A MOTHER AND HER DAUGHTER, WITH A SPRINKLE OF SECRET AGENT EXCITEMENT. GET READY TO DIVE INTO THE ACTION AND UNCOVER THE SURPRISES THAT LIE AHEAD!

TOP SECRET
AGENT AVA GOT A SECRET MISSION:
FIND THE MISSING BIRTHDAY CUPCAKE!

IT WAS HER DAUGHTER LILY'S SPECIAL
DAY. AVA HAD TO ACT FAST.

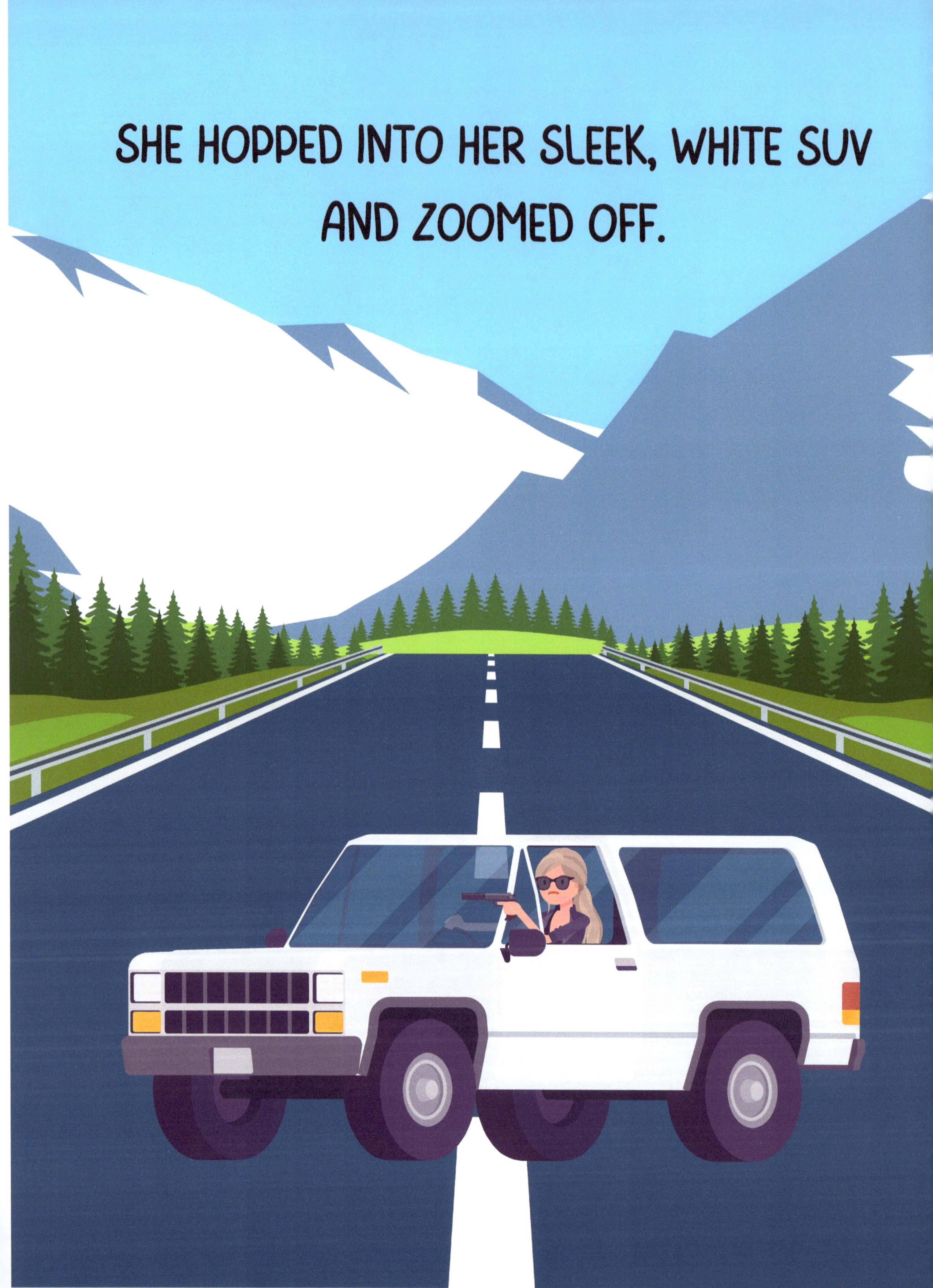

SHE HOPPED INTO HER SLEEK, WHITE SUV
AND ZOOMED OFF.

FIRST STOP, THE BAKERY.

SHE NEEDED CLUES.

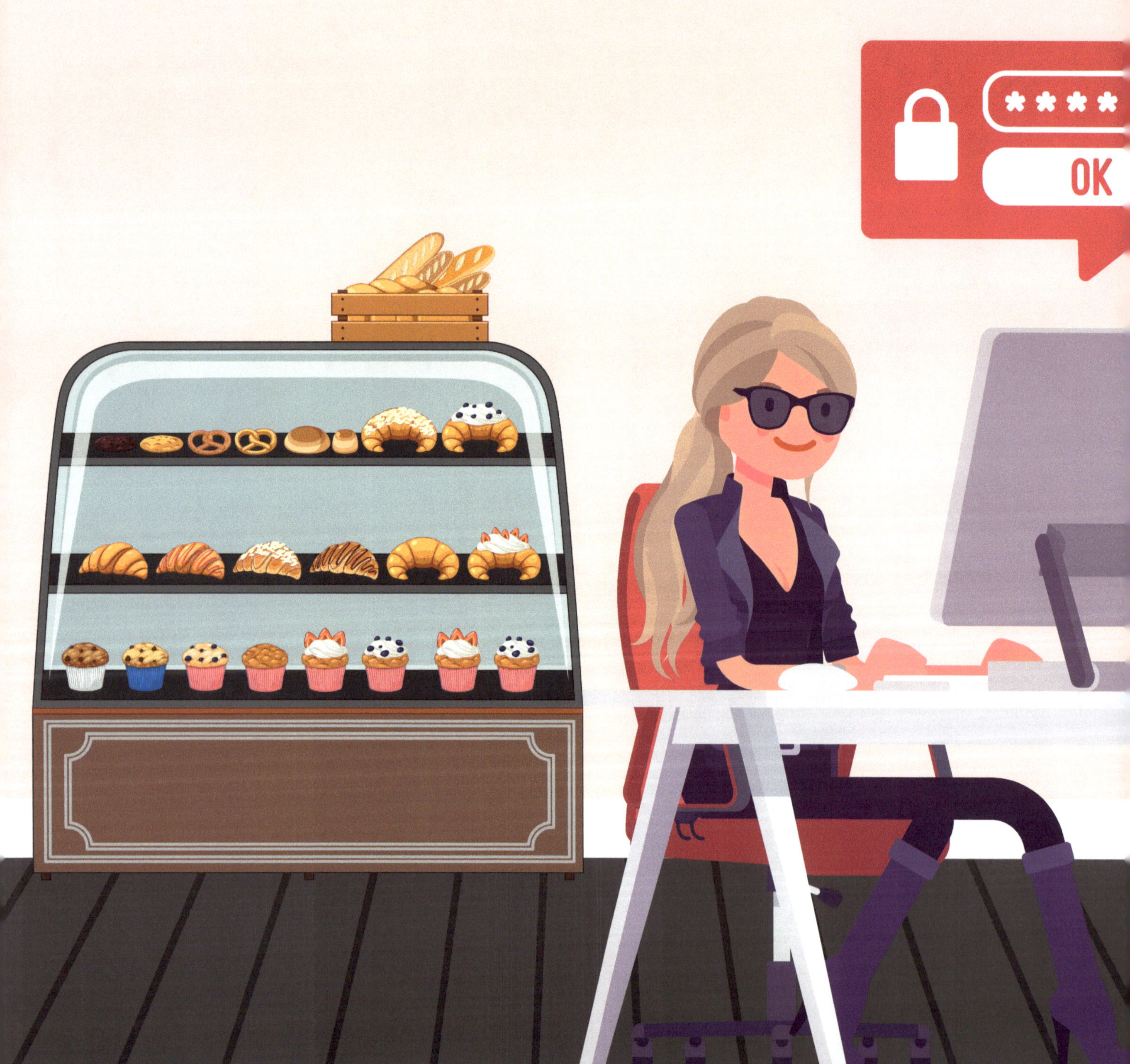

AVA TYPED FURIOUSLY ON HER COMPUTER, SEARCHING BAKERY FILES.
OK

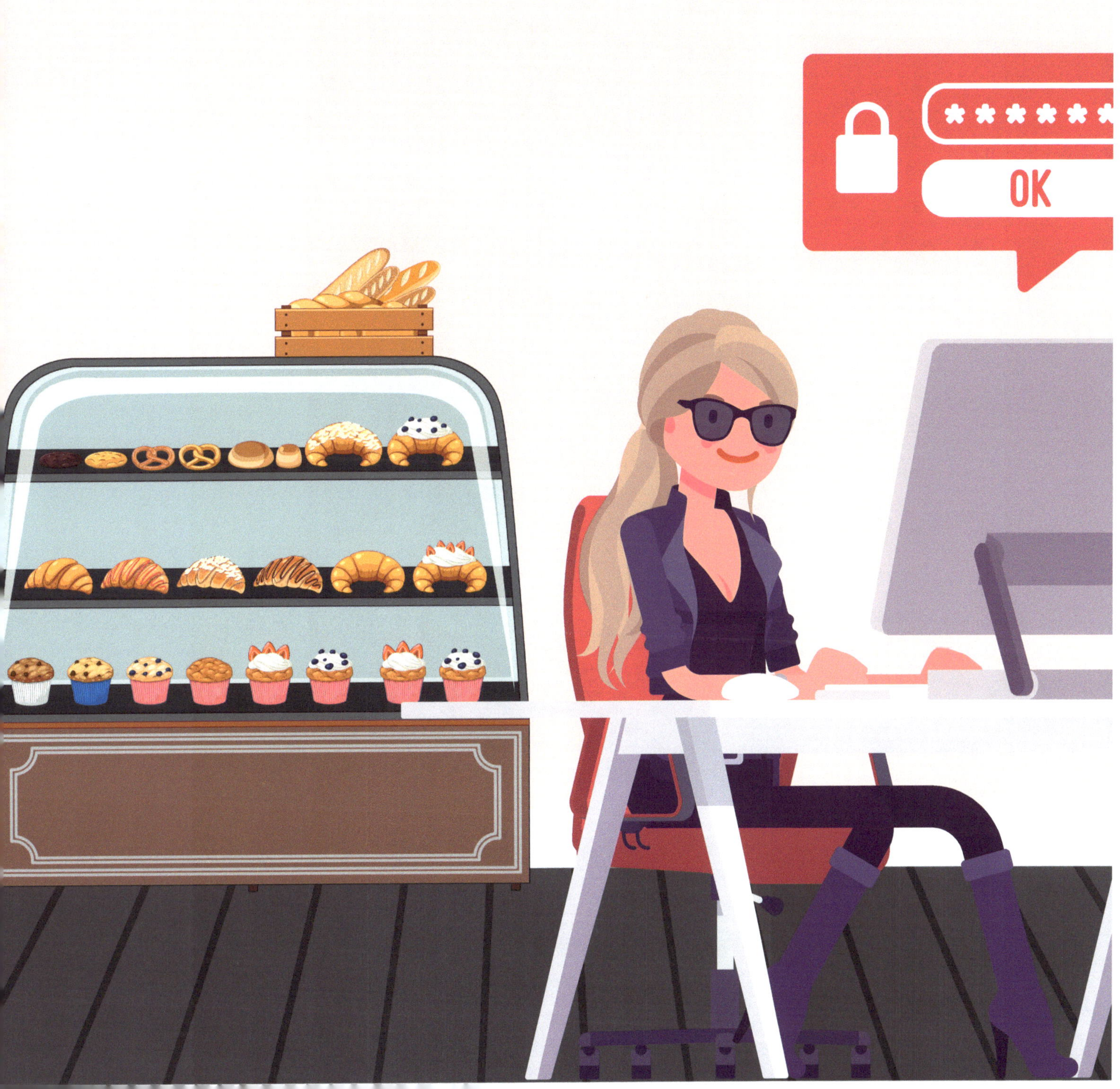

SUDDENLY, SHE HEARD A NOISE BEHIND THE DOOR.
OK

AVA PRESSED HER EAR TO THE DOOR,
LISTENING CAREFULLY.

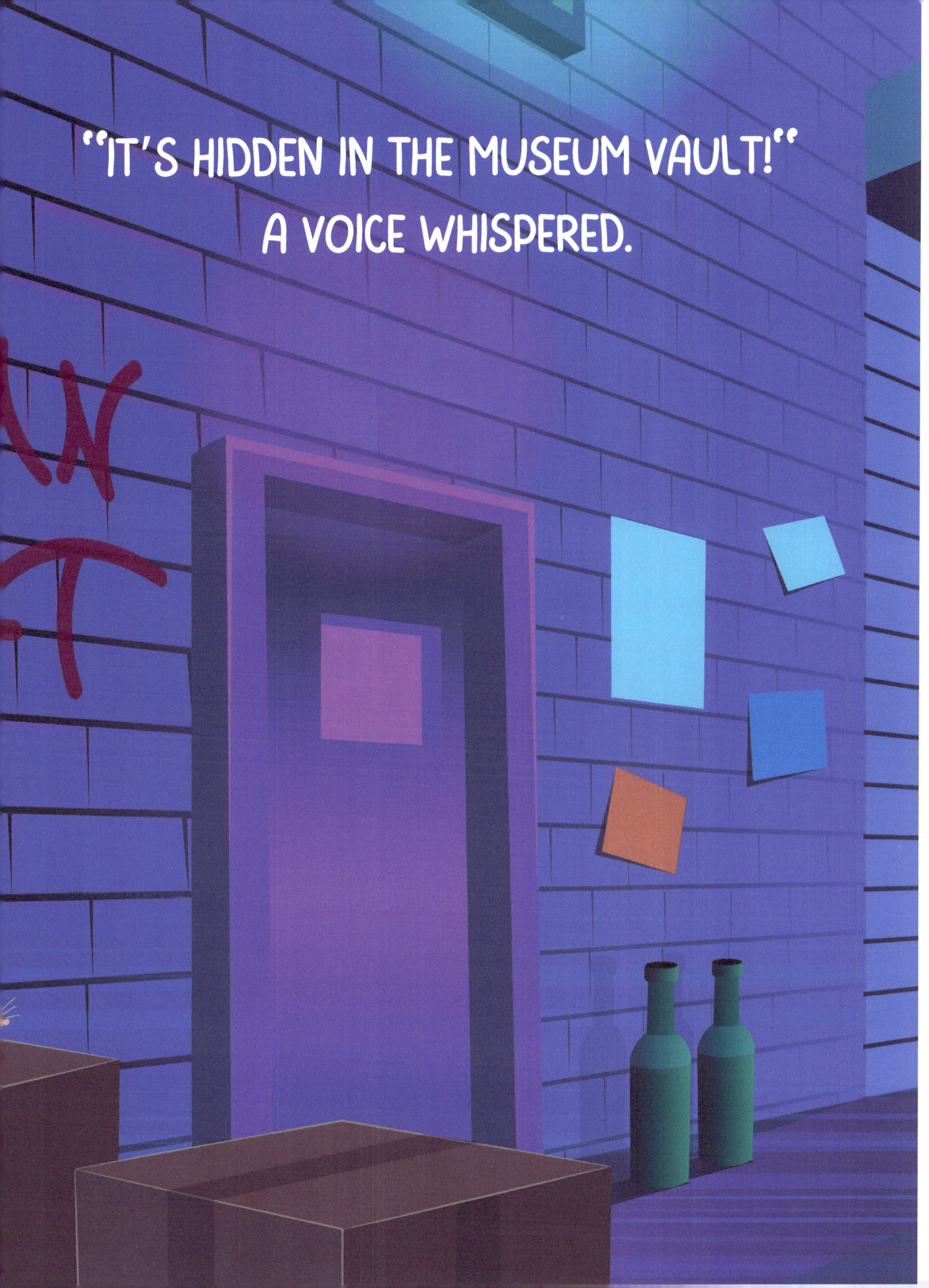
"IT'S HIDDEN IN THE MUSEUM VAULT!"
A VOICE WHISPERED.

HER SIDEKICK MAX GRABBED A GRAPPLING HOOK AND SPECIAL ROPE.
FUN ART

SHE CLIMBED UP THE MUSEUM WALL LIKE A SPIDER.

AT THE TOP, SHE SPRAYED A NON-TOXIC
FORMULA ON THE WINDOW.

THE WINDOW MELTED SILENTLY,
ALLOWING HER TO SLIP INSIDE.

AVA TIPTOED THROUGH THE DARK
HALLWAYS, AVOIDING LASER BEAMS.

SHE REACHED THE VAULT AND BEGAN CRACKING THE SAFE.

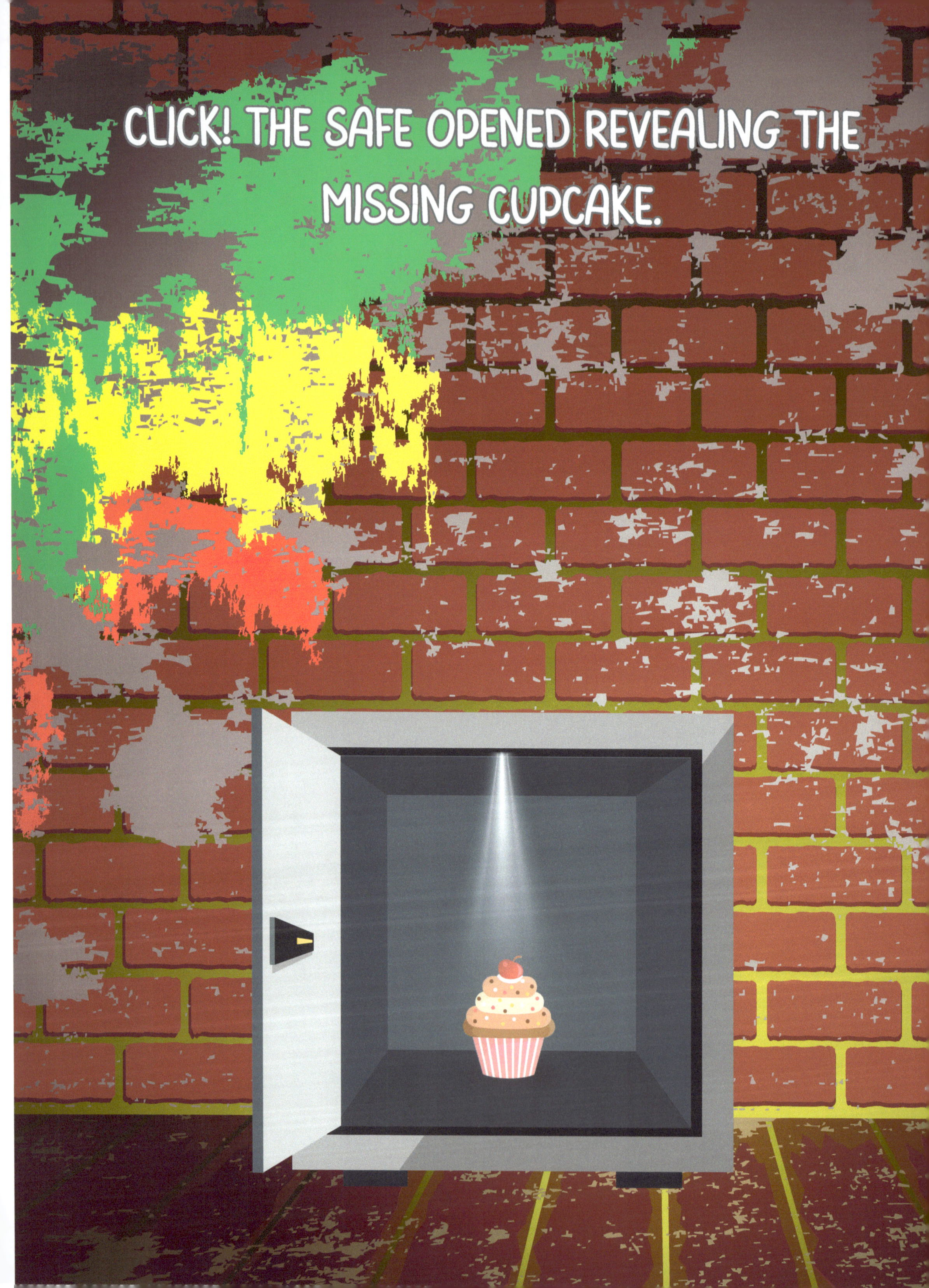

CLICK! THE SAFE OPENED REVEALING THE
MISSING CUPCAKE.

SUDDENLY ALARMS BLARED. AVA GRABBED THE CUPCAKE AND RAN.

SECURITY GUARDS CHASED HER THROUGH THE CORRIDORS.

AVA LEAPED OUT A WINDOW, PULLING HER PARACHUTE CORD.

SHE FLOATED GENTLY TO THE GROUND,
CUPCAKE IN HAND.

A SUV ROARED UP, DRIVEN BY HER SIDEKICK MAX.

AVA JUMPED IN SHOUTING,
"DRIVE MAX DRIVE!"

THEY ZOOMED DOWN THE HIGHWAY PURSUED BY THE GUARDS.
POLICE
PROTECT AND SERVE

AVA LEANED OUT THE WINDOW, SNAPPING PHOTOS FOR EVIDENCE.

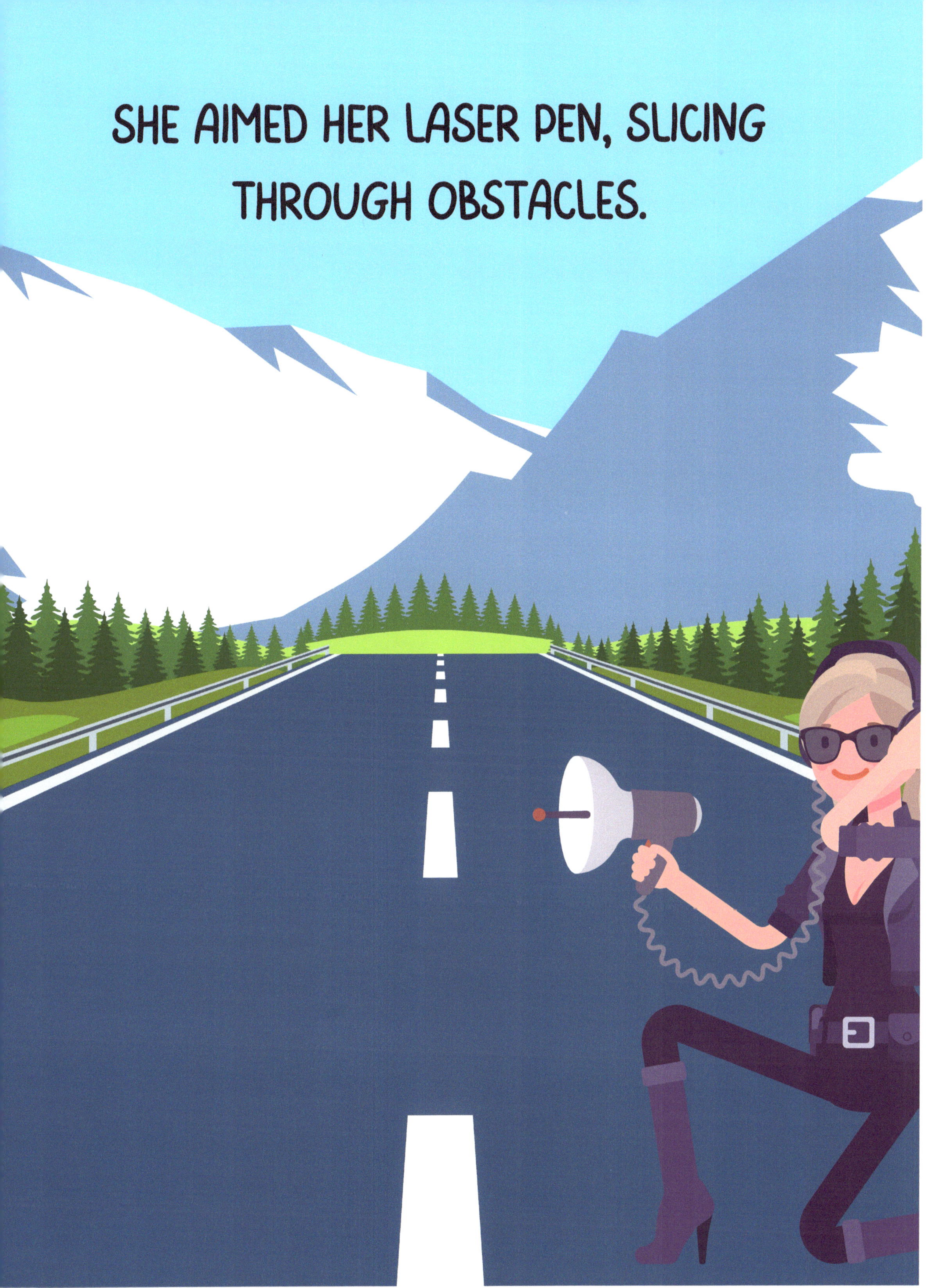

SHE AIMED HER LASER PEN, SLICING THROUGH OBSTACLES.

MAX SWERVED, DODGING THE GUARDS' VEHICLES.
POLICE
PROTECT AND SERVE

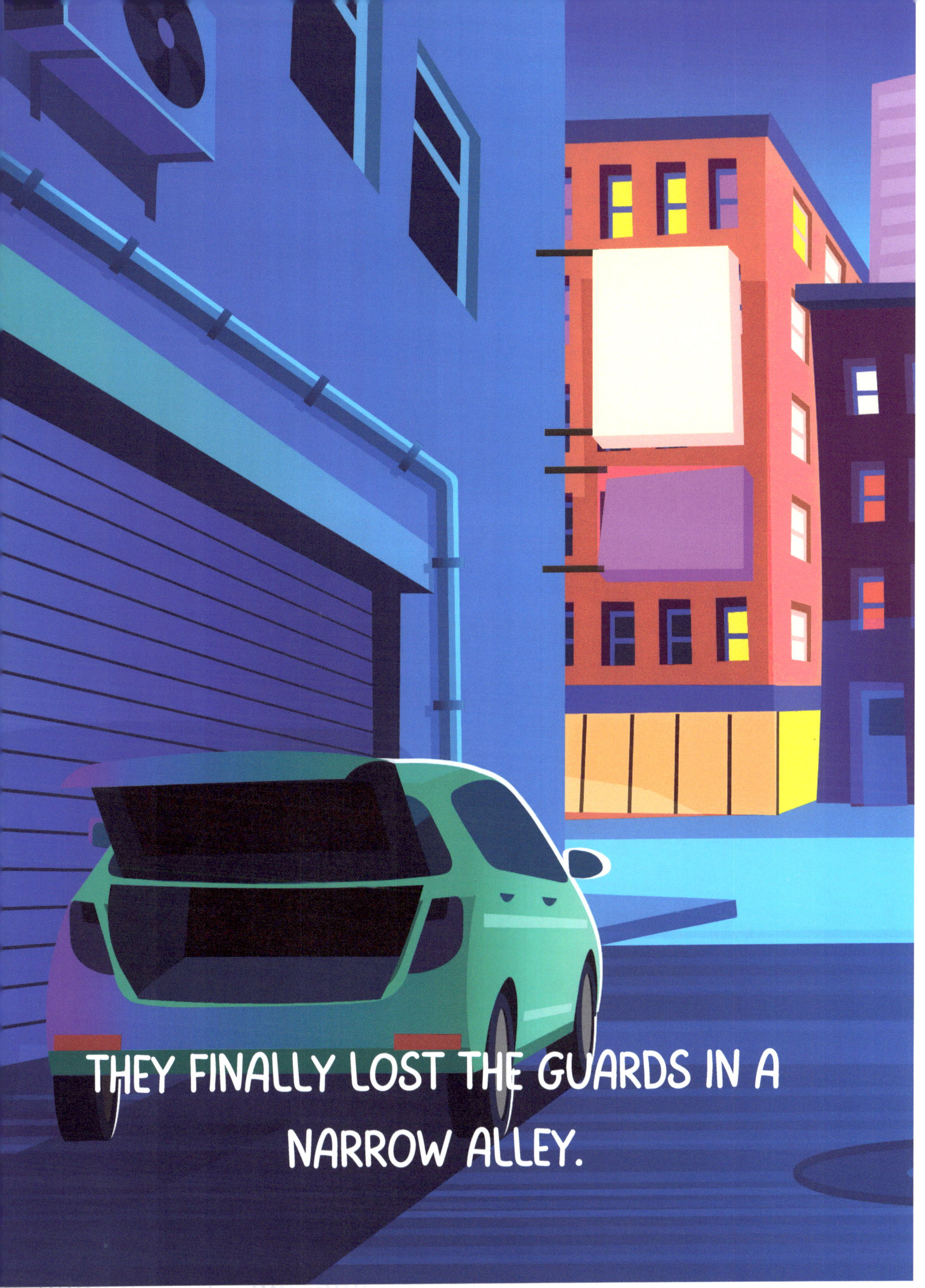

THEY FINALLY LOST THE GUARDS IN A NARROW ALLEY.

AVA CHECKED THE CUPCAKE FOR TRAPS.
IT WAS SAFE.

THEY SPED TO LILY'S PARTY,
MISSION ALMOST COMPLETE.

AVA ARRIVED JUST IN TIME,
HOLDING THE PRECIOUS CUPCAKE.
HAPPY BIRTHDAY

EVERYONE CHEERED AS AVA PLACED THE CUPCAKE ON THE TABLE.

THE PARTY BEGAN, WITH LAUGHTER,
GAMES, AND CAKE.
HAPPY BIRTHDAY

INSIDE THE CUPCAKE, AVA FOUND A CLUE TO HER NEXT MISSION.
HAPPY BIRTHDAY

SHE SMILED, KNOWING ANOTHER
ADVENTURE AWAITED.

ANOTHER MISSION COMPLETED, AGENT
AVA SLEPT SOUNDLY, DREAMING OF
THEIR NEXT ADVENTURE.

THE END

Books By Schaaf

www.BookBySchaaf.com

Find us at: